MARK PODWAL

THE MENORAH STORY

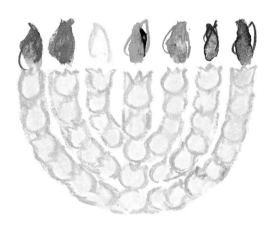

Greenwillow Books, New York

AUTHOR'S NOTE

The seven-branched menorah is the best-known ancient symbol of the Jewish people. The miracle of how the first menorah formed itself can be found in the collection of Jewish legends known as the Midrash Rabbah. In the biblical account, God singled out the skilled artisan Bezalel to fashion the first menorah. According to another legend, King David was victorious in battle because he carried a shield engraved with a prayer in the form of a menorah.

Later, the menorah fell out of favor as the most recognizable symbol of Judaism. There was a Talmudic prohibition against making a copy of the seven-branched Temple menorah. It was also thought that it was too vivid a reminder of the Temple's destruction by the Romans more than two hundred years after the revolt against Antiochus. The Hanukkah menorah, having eight branches, does not violate Talmudic law and recalls the great victory of the Maccabees.

BIBLIOGRAPHY

Ginzberg, Louis. *The Legends of the Jews.* Philadelphia: Jewish Publication Society, 1968.

Goodman, Philip. *The Hanukkah Anthology.* Philadelphia: Jewish Publication Society, 1976.

Yarden, L. *The Tree of Light.* Ithaca: Cornell University Press, 1971.

Gouache and colored pencils were used to create the full-color art. The text type is Romic Light. Copyright © 1998 by Mark Podwal. All rights reserved. No part of this book may be reproduced or utilized in any form or by any means, electronic or mechanical, including photocopying, recording, or by any information storage and retrieval system, without permission in writing from the Publisher, Greenwillow Books, a division of William Morrow & Company, Inc., 1350 Avenue of the Americas, New York, NY 10019. www.williammorrow.com   Printed in Singapore by Tien Wah Press   First Edition 10 9 8 7 6 5 4 3 2 1

Library of Congress Cataloging-in-Publication Data: Podwal, Mark H. (date)   The menorah story / by Mark Podwal.   p.   cm. Includes bibliographical references.   Summary: Discusses the story of the Hanukkah menorah which commemorates the miraculous victory of the Maccabees over King Antiochus and his army.   ISBN 0-688-15758-0 (trade).   ISBN 0-688-15759-9 (lib. bdg.) 1. Menorah—Legends—Juvenile literature.   [1. Menorah.   2. Jews—History—586 B.C.–70 A.D.   3. Hanukkah.]   1. Title. BM657.M35P63   1998   296.4'61—dc21   97-36300   CIP   AC

For Michael Zohar

God tried many times to teach Moses how to make a menorah. But whenever Moses set about making one, he couldn't remember what it was supposed to look like. God even drew a picture of a menorah on Moses' palm and told him to copy it. Still, Moses could not do it. So God told Moses to throw a piece of gold into a fire. And the first menorah formed itself.

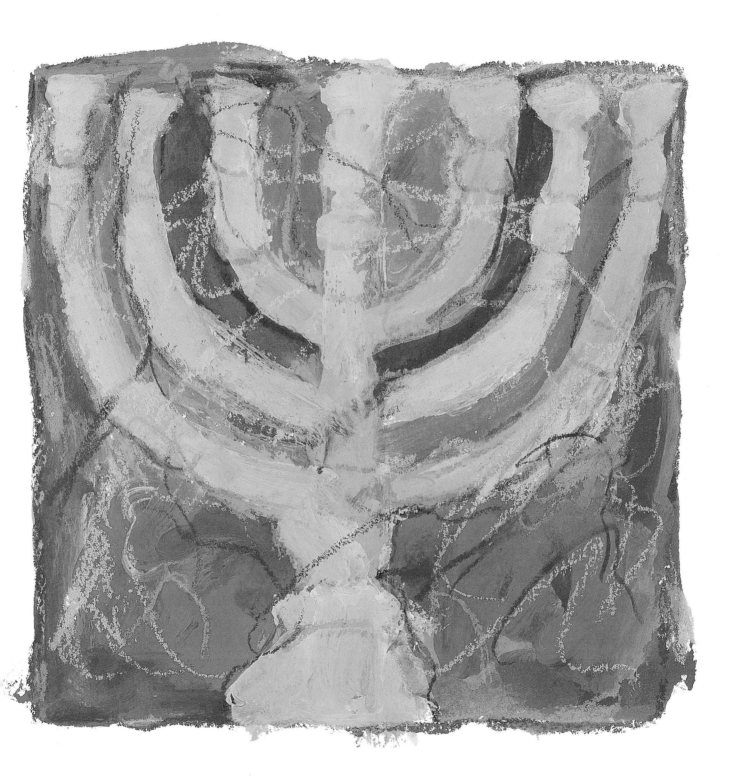

It was said that the menorah's seven lights symbolized the six days of Creation with the light in the center representing the Sabbath, the day of rest.

Some believed the menorah symbolized the glow of the planets as they followed their paths through the heavens.

Others thought the seven flames represented the seven continents of the earth.

For hundreds of years a golden menorah burned day and night at the center of the Holy Temple, which was at the center of the city of Jerusalem, which was at the center of the world.

But there came a time when the lights of the menorah went out.

It was in the days of the wicked King Antiochus's rule over Israel. The king commanded everyone in his realm to pray only to the Greek gods. When the Jews refused, Antiochus ordered his soldiers to tear down the gates and towers that protected Jerusalem. Idols were placed inside the Holy Temple.

A law was passed forbidding the Jews to say God's name.
Holy scrolls were torn to shreds and burned.

The golden menorah was hidden from Antiochus's soldiers
so it would not be carried off with all the other treasures of
the Holy Temple.

Jewish families left their homes and all their possessions. They escaped to the mountains, where they lived in caves and formed an army. At night, from the hills, they would attack the enemy, taking them by surprise. And throughout the land, Jews smashed the idols.

King Antiochus, determined to defeat the Jews, gathered together his entire army. The ground shook from the weight of enormous elephants that carried on their backs towers filled with soldiers. So confident was Antiochus of victory that he brought along slave dealers to whom he promised to sell captured Jews for very little.

When the Jews saw how few they were against so many, there was great anguish throughout Israel.

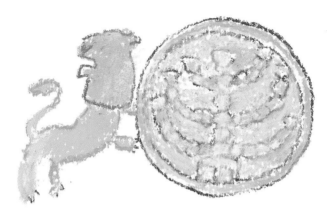

But Judah Maccabee, the leader of the Jews, told his people not to fear the enemy's numbers. He reminded them of how their ancestors had been saved from Pharaoh's army when God split the Red Sea. He said that God would help them again.

And a miracle did happen. An angel of God appeared, dressed in golden armor and holding a fiery sword, filling the horizon.

Their courage strengthened, the Jews defeated the mighty army of Antiochus.

From all over the land of Israel the people came to rebuild Jerusalem. Palm branches were carried by hands that had carried swords.

The idols were removed. The stones and pillars of the Holy Temple were restored and polished. High walls and strong towers were built around the city so that no enemy could destroy Jerusalem again.

Accompanied by songs and harps and cymbals, the golden menorah was brought from its hiding place and carried to the Holy Temple.

Only a small amount of holy oil, hardly enough to burn
for a single day, could be found to light the menorah. Yet,
miraculously, the menorah burned for *eight* days, which
was all the time needed to prepare new holy oil.

And so Judah Maccabee proclaimed an eight-day holiday called Hanukkah, as a time of rejoicing for future generations.

Not surprisingly, Hanukkah menorahs are made with eight lights, though sometimes a "servant light" is added to kindle the holy flames.

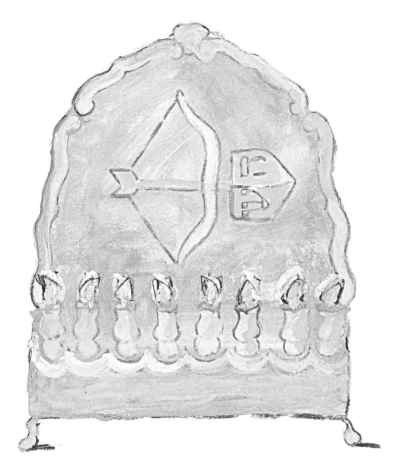

Each year during Hanukkah, menorahs are lit and placed in the doorways and windows of Jewish homes and synagogues. Unlike the lights of the seven-branched menorah that recall the days of Creation or the continents of the earth, these eight small lights celebrate great miracles of long ago.